John Hookham Frere

The Birds of Aristophanes

John Hookham Frere

The Birds of Aristophanes

ISBN/EAN: 9783337008598

Printed in Europe, USA, Canada, Australia, Japan

Cover: Foto ©Thomas Meinert / pixelio.de

More available books at **www.hansebooks.com**

THE BIRDS OF ARISTOPHANES.

TRANSLATED BY

JOHN HOOKHAM FRERE.

Cambridge:
PRINTED FOR THE COMMITTEE AT THE UNIVERSITY PRESS;
AND SOLD BY
MACMILLAN & BOWES.
1883
[*All Rights reserved.*]

PREFACE.

IN this Edition the text of Mr Frere has been arranged in conformity with the acting-edition of the Greek Text; and the pages have been numbered to correspond with the pages of that edition. In a few passages, where Mr Frere adopts a different distribution of the words among the characters, his arrangement is indicated by the names enclosed in square brackets; as on pages 20, 36, 37, 39.

The translation of the Parabasis by Mr Swinburne, which appeared in *The Athenæum*, 30th October, 1880, has, by the kind permission of the proprietors of that Journal, been printed at the end of Mr Frere's version.

J. W. C.

November, 1883.

DRAMATIS PERSONÆ.

PEITHETAIRUS, an Athenian citizen, but disgusted with his own country, starts on his travels proposing to seek his fortune in the kingdom of the Birds. He is represented as the essential man of business and ability, the true political adventurer; the man who directs every thing and every body; who is never in the wrong, never at a loss, never satisfied with what has been done by others, uniformly successful in his operations. He maintains a constant ascendency, or if he loses it for a moment, recovers it immediately.

Euelpides, a simple easy-minded droll companion, his natural follower and adherent; as the Merry Andrew is of the Mountebank. It will be seen that, like the Merry Andrew, he interposes his buffoonish comments on the grand oration delivered by his master.

Epops, King of the Birds; formerly Tereus, King of Thrace, but long ago, according to the records of mythology, transformed into a *Hoopoe*. He appears as the courteous dignified sovereign of a primitive uncivilized race, whom he is desirous to improve: he gives a gracious reception to strangers arriving from a country more advanced in civilization; and adopts the projects of aggrandizement suggested to him by Peithetairus.

The Chorus of Birds, his subjects, retain, on the contrary, their hereditary hatred and suspicion of the human race; they are ready to break out into open mutiny against their king, and to massacre his foreign (human) advisers upon the spot. It is with the greatest difficulty that they can be prevailed upon to hear reason, and attend to the luminous exposition of Peithetairus. His harangue has the effect of conciliating and convincing them; his projects are adopted without a dissentient voice. War is not immediately declared against the gods, but a sort of Mexican blockade is established by proclamation.

Prometheus, a malcontent deity, the ancient patron of the human race, still retaining a concealed attachment to the deposed dynasty of Saturn. He comes over secretly with intelligence, which Peithetairus avails himself of, and which proves ultimately decisive of the subjugation of the gods.

Neptune, Hercules, Triballus, or the *Triballian,* } joint ambassadors from the gods, commissioned to treat with Peithetairus. *Neptune* is represented as a formal dignified personage of the old school; *Hercules* as a passionate, wrong-headed, greedy blockhead: he is cajoled and gained over by Peithetairus; and in his turn intimidates the *Triballian,* an ignorant barbarian deity, who is hardly able to speak intelligibly. They join together, Neptune is out-voted, and Peithetairus concludes a treaty by which his highest pretensions are realized.

The characters above mentioned are the only ones who contribute in any way to the progress of the drama; the remainder, a very amusing set of persons, are introduced in detached scenes, exemplifying the various interruptions and annoyances incident to the man of business, distracting his attention and embarrassing him in the exercise of his authoritative functions. There are, however, exceptions,—

Iris, who is brought in, having been captured and detained for an infringement of the blockade.

A Priest who comes to sacrifice at the inauguration of the new city.

Two Messengers arriving from different quarters, with very interesting and satisfactory intelligence.

The rest are a mere series of intruders on the time and attention of the great man.

A Poet, a ragged vagabond, who comes begging with an inaugural ode on the foundation of the new city.

A Soothsayer, arriving with oracles relative to the same important event, and a demand of perquisites due to himself by divine authority.

Meton, the Astronomer, proposes to make a plan and survey of the new city.

A Commissioner from Athens, a very authoritative personage.

A Vendor of copies of decrees: he enters, reading them aloud, like a hawker to attract purchasers.

A Parricide, a young man who has beaten his father, and proposes to strangle him, offers himself as a desirable acquisition to the new colony.

An Informer, a young man whose hereditary trade is that of an informer, and whose practice extends to the Islands, comes with the same application.

ACT I.

SCENE: *a wild desolate country with a bare open prospect on one side, and some rocks covered with shrubs and brushwood in the centre of the stage. Enter Peithetairus and Euelpides the one with a Raven and the other with a Jackdaw on his hand.*

Euelpides (speaking to his Jackdaw).

IGHT on, do ye say? to the tree there in the distance?
    Pei. (*speaking first to his Raven, and then to his companion*). Plague take ye! Why, this creature calls us back!

    Eu. What use can it answer tramping up and down? We're lost, I tell ye: our journey's come to nothing.

    Pei. To think of me travelling a thousand stadia With a Raven for my adviser!

    Eu.   Think of me too, Going at the instigation of a Jackdaw, To wear my toes and my toe-nails to pieces!

    Pei. I don't know even the country, where we've got to.

    Eu. And yet you expect to find a country here,   10
A country for yourself!

    Pei.   Truly, not I;
Not even Execestides could do it,
That finds himself a native every where.

    Eu. Oh dear! We're come to ruin, utter ruin!

    Pei. Then go that way, can't ye?--the "Road to Ruin!"

Eu. He has brought us to a fine pass, that crazy fellow
Philocrates the poulterer; he pretended
To enable us to find where Tereus lives;
The King that was, the Hoopoe that is now;
Persuading us to buy these creatures of him,
That Raven there for three-pence, and this other,—
This little Tharrelides of a Jackdaw,—
He charged a penny for: but neither of 'em
Are fit for any thing but to bite and scratch.
   (*Speaking to his Jackdaw.*)
Well, what are ye after now? gaping and poking!   20
You've brought us straight to the rock. Where would you
    take us?
There's no road here!
   Pei.   No, none, not even a path.
   Eu. Nor don't your Raven tell us any thing?
   Pei. She's alter'd somehow—she croaks differently.
   Eu. But which way does she point? What does she say?
   Pei. Say? Why, she says, she'll bite my fingers off.
   Eu. Well, truly it's hard upon us, hard indeed,
To go with our own carcases to the crows,
And not be able to find 'em after all.
   (*Turning to the audience.*)
For our design, most excellent spectators,   30
(Our passion, our disease, or what you will,)
Is the reverse of that which Sacas feels;
For he, though not a native, strives perforce
To make himself a citizen: whilst we,
Known and acknowledg'd as Athenians born,
(Not hustled off, nor otherwise compell'd,)
Have deem'd it fitting to betake ourselves
To these our legs, and make our person scarce.

Not through disgust or hatred or disdain
Of our illustrious birth-place, which we deem
Glorious and free; with equal laws ordain'd
For fine and forfeiture and confiscation;
With taxes universally diffused;
And suits and pleas abounding in the Courts.
  For grasshoppers sit only for a month
Chirping upon the twigs; but our Athenians   40
Sit chirping and discussing all the year,
Perch'd upon points of evidence and law.
  Therefore we trudge upon our present travels,
With these our sacrificial implements,
To seek some easier unlitigious place,
Meaning to settle there and colonize.
Our present errand is in search of Tereus,
(The Hoopoe that is now) to learn from him
If in his expeditions, flights, and journeys,
He ever chanced to light on such a spot.
    Pei.   Holloh!
    Eu.   What's that?
    Pei.   My raven here points upwards.
—Decidedly!   50
    Eu.   Ay, and here's my Jackdaw, too,
Gaping as if she saw something above.—
Yes, I'll be bound for it; this must be the place:
We'll make a noise, and know the truth of it.
    Pei.   Then "kick against the rock."
    Eu.   Knock you your head
Against the rock!—and make it a double knock!
    Pei.   Then fling a stone at it!

Eu.   With all my heart,
Holloh, there!
    Pei.   What do you mean with your Holloh?
You should cry Hoop for a Hoopoe.
    Eu.   Well, then, Hoop!
Hoop and holloh, there!—Hoopoe, Hoopoe, I say!   60
    Trochilus. What's here? Who's bawling there? Who wants
        my master?

The door is opened, and both parties start at seeing each other.

    Eu. Oh mercy, mighty Apollo! what a beak!
    Tr. Out! out upon it! a brace of bird-catchers!
    Eu. Now tell me, in heaven's name, what creature are ye?
    Tr. I'm a Slave Bird.   70
    Eu.   A slave! how did it happen?
Were you made prisoner by a fighting cock?
    Tr. No. When my master made himself a Hoopoe,
He begg'd me to turn bird to attend upon him.
    Eu. Do birds, then, want attendance?
    Tr.   Yes, of course;
In his case, having been a man before,
He longs occasionally for human diet,
His old Athenian fare: pilchards for instance,—
Then I must fetch the pilchards; sometimes porridge;
He calls for porridge, and I mix it for him.
    Eu. Well, you're a dapper waiter, a Didapper;

But, Didapper, I say, do step within there,
And call your master out.
 Tr.   But just at present
He's taking a little rest after his luncheon,
Some myrtle berries and a dish of worms.
 Eu. No matter, call him here; we wish to speak to him.
 Tr. He'll not be pleas'd, I'm sure; but, notwithstanding,
Since you desire it, I'll make bold to call him. [*Exit.*
 Pei. (*looking after him*). Confound ye, I say, you've frighten'd me to death.
 Eu. He has scared away my Jackdaw; it's flown away.
 Pei. You let it go yourself, you coward.
 Eu.   Tell me,
Have not you let your Raven go?
 Pei.   Not I.
 Eu. Where is it then?
 Pei.   Flown off of its own accord.
 Eu. You did not let it go! you're a brave fellow!
 The Hoopoe (*from within*). Open the door, I say; let me go forth.

 The Royal Hoopoe appears with a tremendous beak and crest.

 Eu. O Hercules, what a creature! What a plumage!

And a triple tier of crests; what can it be!
 Hoo. Who call'd? who wanted me?
 Eu.   May the heavenly powers—
Confound ye! I say (*aside*).
 Hoo.   You mock at me, perhaps,
Seeing these plumes.—But, stranger, you must know
That once I was a man.
 Eu.   We did not laugh
At you, Sir.
 Hoo. What, then, were you laughing at?
 Eu. Only that beak of yours seem'd rather odd.
 Hoo. It was your poet Sophocles that reduced me 100
To this condition with his tragedies.
 Eu. What are you, Tereus? Are you a bird, or what?
 Hoo. A bird.
 Eu.   Then where are all your feathers?
 Hoo.   Gone.
 Eu. In consequence of an illness?
 Hoo.   No; the Birds
At this time of the year leave off their feathers.
But you; what are ye? Tell me.
 Eu.   Mortal men.
 Hoo. What countrymen?
 Eu.   Of the country of the Triremes[1].
 Hoo. Jurymen, I suppose?

---

[1] Athens, mistress of the sea.

Eu.   Quite the reverse,
We're anti-jurymen.
    Hoo.   Does that breed still
Continue amongst you?
    Eu.   Some few specimens
You'll meet with, here and there, in country places.
    Hoo.   And what has brought you here? What was your object?
    Eu.   We wish'd to advise with you.
    Hoo.   With me! For what?
    Eu.   Because you were a man, the same as us;
And found yourself in debt, the same as us;
And did not like to pay, the same as us;
And after that, you changed into a bird,
And ever since have flown and wander'd far
Over the lands and seas, and have acquir'd
All knowledge that a bird or man can learn.
    Therefore we come, as suppliants, to beseech
Your favour and advice to point us out
Some comfortable country, close and snug,
A country like a blanket or a rug,
Where we might fairly fold ourselves to rest.
    Hoo.   Do you wish then for a greater state than Athens?
    Eu.   Not greater, but more suitable for us.
    Hoo.   It's clear you're fond of aristocracy.
    Eu.   What, him, the son of Scellias! Aristocrates?
I abhor him.
    Hoo.   Well, what kind of a town would suit ye?
    Eu.   Why, such a kind of town as this, for instance,
A town where the importunities and troubles

Are of this sort. Suppose a neighbour calls
Betimes in the morning with a sudden summons:
"Now, don't forget," says he, "for heaven's sake,   130
To come to me to-morrow; bring your friends,
Children, and all, we've wedding cheer at home.
Come early, mind ye, and if you fail me now,
Don't let me see your face when I'm in trouble."
    Hoo. Ay! You're in love, I see, with difficulties
And miseries. Well, there's a city, in fact,
Much of this sort; one that I think might suit ye,
Near the Red Sea.   145
    Eu.   No, no! not near the sea!
Lest I should have the Salaminian galley
Arriving some fine morning with a summons
Sent after me, and a poursuivant to arrest me.
    But tell me, among the birds here, how do ye find it?   155
What kind of an existence?
    Hoo.   Pretty fair;
Not much amiss. Time passes smoothly enough;
And money is out of the question. We don't use it.
    Eu. You've freed yourselves from a great load of dross.
    Hoo. We've our field sports. We spend our idle mornings
With banqueting and collations in the gardens,
With poppy seeds and myrtle.   160
    Eu.   So your time
Is pass'd like a perpetual wedding-day.
    Peithetairus breaks out as from a profound reverie.
    Pei. Hah! What a power is here; what opportunities!
If I could only advise you; I see it all!
The means for an infinite empire and command!
    Hoo. And what would you have us do? What's your advice?

ACT I.

Pei. Do! what would I have ye do? Why, first of all
Don't flutter and hurry about all open-mouth'd
In that undignified way.
    Hoo.   What then?
    Pei. (emphatically).   Concentrate;
Bring all your birds together. Build a city.
    Hoo. The birds! How could we build a city? Where?
    Pei. Nonsense. You can't be serious. What a question!
Look down.   175
    Hoo.   I do.
    Pei.   Look up now.
    Hoo.   So I do.
    Pei. Now turn your neck round.
    Hoo.   I should sprain it though.
    Pei. Come, what d'ye see?
    Hoo.   The clouds and sky;—that's all.
    Pei. Well, that we call the pole and the atmosphere;
And would it not serve you birds for a metropole?
Well, there then, you may build and fortify,
And call it your metropolis,—your acropolis.
From that position you'll command mankind,   185
And keep them in utter thorough subjugation:
Just as you do the grasshoppers and locusts.
And if the gods offend you, you'll blockade 'em,
And starve 'em to a surrender.
    Hoo.   In what way?
    Pei. Why thus. Your atmosphere is plac'd, you see,
In a middle point, just betwixt earth and heaven.
  A case of the same kind occurs with us.
Our people in Athens, if they send to Delphi
With deputations, offerings, or what not,
Are forced to obtain a pass from the Bœotians:

Thus, when mankind on earth are sacrificing,
If you should find the gods grown mutinous
And insubordinate, you could intercept
All their supplies of sacrificial smoke.
 Hoo. By the earth and all its springs! springes and nooses!
Odds nets and snares! this is the cleverest notion: 195
And I could find it in my heart to venture,
If the other Birds agree to the proposal.
 Pei. But who must state it to them?
 Hoo.   You yourself:
They'll understand ye, I found them mere barbarians;
But living here a length of time amongst them,
I have taught them to converse and speak correctly.   200
 Pei. How will you summon them?
 Hoo.   That's easy enough;
I'll just step into the thicket here hard by,
And call my Nightingale. She'll summon them.
And when they hear her voice, I promise you
You'll see them all come running here pell mell.
 Pei. My dearest, best of birds! don't lose a moment,
I beg, but go directly into the thicket;
Nay, don't stand here, go call your Nightingale.
              [*Exit Hoopoe.*

SONG, *from behind the scene, supposed to be sung by the Hoopoe.*

    Awake! awake!
  Sleep no more, my gentle mate!
  With your tiny tawny bill,   210
  Wake the tuneful echo shrill,
    On vale or hill;

ACT I.

Or in her airy rocky seat,
Let her listen and repeat
The tender ditty that you tell,
    The sad lament,
    The dire event,
To luckless Itys that befell.
    Thence the strain
    Shall rise again,
    And soar amain,
Up to the lofty palace gate,
Where mighty Apollo sits in state
In Jove's abode, with his ivory lyre,
Hymning aloud to the heavenly quire;
While all the gods shall join with thee
    In a celestial symphony.

A solo on the flute supposed to be the Nightingale's call.

Pei. Oh, Jupiter! the dear delicious bird!
With what a lovely tone she swells and falls,
Sweetening the wilderness with delicate air.
    Eu. Hist!
    Pei.   What?
    Eu.   Be quiet, can't ye!
    Pei.   What's the matter?
    Eu. The Hoopoe is just preparing for a song.
    Hoo.   Hoop! hoop!
        Come in a troop,
        Come at a call,
          One and all,
        Birds of a feather,
        All together.
    Birds of an humble gentle bill
        Smooth and shrill,
Dieted on seeds and grain,

Rioting on the furrow'd plain,
  Pecking, hopping,
  Picking, popping,
Among the barley newly sown.
  Birds of bolder louder tone,
    Lodging in the shrubs and bushes,
    Mavises and Thrushes,
On the summer berries browsing,
On the garden fruits carousing,
All the grubs and vermin smouzing.

You that in an humbler station,
With an active occupation,
Haunt the lowly watery mead,
Warring against the native breed,
The gnats and flies, your enemies;
In the level marshy plain
Of Marathon pursued and slain.

You that in a squadron driving   250
From the seas are seen arriving,
With the Cormorants and Mews
Haste to land and hear the news!
  All the feather'd airy nation,
Birds of every size and station,
Are conven'd in convocation.
    For an envoy queer and shrewd
    Means to address the multitude,
And submit to their decision
A surprising proposition,
For the welfare of the state.

> Come in a flurry,
> With a hurry, scurry,
> Hurry to the meeting and attend to the debate.

At this point Mr Frere omits about forty lines; and his remarks are interesting enough to occupy worthily the gap thus made in the text.

The first appearance of the Chorus must have been a critical point for the success of a play. The audience had been brought into good humour by their favourite musical performer, by whom all the preceding songs were probably executed; for the dialogue on the stage passes solely between Peithetairus and Euelpides, and the Hoopoe, who is supposed to sing, does not appear. The Chorus now comes on, and in the original, forty lines follow, in which Peithetairus and Euelpides act as showmen to the exhibition of twenty-four figures, dressed in imitation of the plumage of as many different kinds of birds, which are passed in review with suitable remarks as they successively take their places in the orchestra. This passage is here omitted. Whoever wishes to see how well it can be executed, may be referred to Mr Cary's translation.

The passage in question is much shortened for the present performance, and the entry of the Birds is illustrated by some characteristic ballet-music, which will speak for itself.

While the Birds are bustling about in their new coop of the orchestra, Euelpides contemplates them with surprise, which soon changes to alarm.

The language of the Birds consists almost entirely of short syllables, the effect of which it is almost impossible to imitate in English. Some accents, which are added, may serve to make the attempt; they are added also to two spondaic lines, of which the imitation is more practicable.

Eu. How they thicken, how they muster,
How they clutter, how they cluster!
Now they ramble here and ·thither,
Now they scramble altogether.
What a fidgetting and clattering!
What a twittering and chattering!
Don't they mean to threaten us? What think ye?
   Pei.   Yes, methinks they do.
   Eu. They're gaping with an angry look against us both.
   Pei.   It's very true.
   Eu. Where is He, the Màgistrate that assèmbled us to deliberate?   310
   Hoo. Friends and comrades, here am I, your old associate and ally.
   Cho. What have ye to commùnicate for the bènefit of the stàte?
   Hoo. A proposal safe and useful, practicable, profitable,

Two projectors are arriv'd here, politicians shrewd and able.
 Cho. Whee! whaw! where! where!
What? what? what? what? what?
 Hoo. I repeat it—human envoys are arrived, a steady pair, 320
To disclose without reserve a most stupendous huge affair.
 Cho. Chief, of all that ever were, the worst, the most unhappy one!
Speak, explain!
 Hoo.   Don't be alarm'd!
 Cho.   Alas, alas! what have you done?
 Hoo. I've received a pair of strangers, who desired to settle here.
 Cho. Have you risk'd so rash an act?
 Hoo.   I've done it, and I persevere.
 Cho. But where are they?
 Hoo.   Near beside you; near as I am; very near.
 Cho.   Oùt, alàs! oùt, alàs!
We are betrày'd, cruelly betray'd
To a calàmitous end.
Our còmrade and our friènd,
Our compànion in the fièlds and in the pàstures
Is the aùthor of all our mìseries and dìsasters.
Our àncient sàcred làws and sòlemn oàth! 330
Trànsgrèssing bòth!
Trèasonably delìvering us as a prìze
To our hòrrible immemòrial enemiès,
To a detèstable race
Exècrably base!
For the Bird our Chief, hereafter he must answer to the State;
With respect to these intruders, I propose, without debate,

On the spot to tear and hack them.
Eu.   There it is, our death and ruin!
Ah, the fault was all your own, you know it; it was all your
    doing;
You that brought me here, and why?   340
  Pei.   Because I wanted an attendant.
  Eu.   Here to close my life in tears.
  Pei.   No, that's a foolish fear, depend on't.
  Eu.   Why a foolish fear?
  Pei.   Consider; when you're left without an eye,
It's impossible in nature; how could you contrive to cry?
  Cho.   Form in rank; form in rank;
               Then move forward and outflank.
               Let me see them overpower'd,
               Hack'd, demolish'd, and devour'd,   350
               Neither earth, nor sea, nor sky,
               Nor woody fastnesses on high,
               Shall protect them if they fly.
Where's the Captain? what detains him? what prevents us to
    proceed?
On the right there, call the Captain! let him form his troop
    and lead.
  Eu.   There it is; where can I fly?
  Pei.   Sirrah, be quiet; wait a bit.
  Eu.   What, to be devour'd amongst them!

Pei. Will your legs or will your wit serve to escape them?
Eu. I can't tell.
Pei. But I can tell; do as you're bid;
Fight we must. You see the pot, just there before ye; take the lid,
And present it for a shield; the spit will serve you for a spear; 360
With it you may scare them off, or spike them if they venture near.
Eu. What can I find to guard my eyes?
Pei. Why, there's the very thing you wish,
Two vizard helmets ready made, the cullender and skimming dish.
Eu. What a clever, capital, lucky device, sudden and new!
Nicias, with all his tactics, is a simpleton to you.
Cho. Steady, Birds! present your beaks! in double time, charge and attack!
Pounce upon them, smash the potlid, clapperclaw them, tear and hack.
Hoo. Tell me, most unworthy creatures, scandal of the feather'd race,
Must I see my friends and kinsmen massacred before my face?
Cho. What, do you propose to spare them? Where will your forbearance cease,
Hesitating to destroy destructive creatures such as these? 370
Hoo. Enemies they might have been; but here they come, with fair design,
With proposals of advice, for your advantage and for mine.
Cho. Enemies time out of mind! they that have spilt our fathers' blood,
How should they be friends of ours, or give us counsel for our good?

Hoo. Friendship is a poor adviser; politicians deep and wise
Many times are forc'd to learn a lesson from their enemies;
Diligent and wary conduct is the method soon or late
Which an adversary teaches; whilst a friend or intimate
Trains us on to sloth and ease; to ready confidence; to rest
In a careless acquiescence; to believe and hope the best.
Look on earth! behold the nations, all in emulation vying,
Active all, with busy science engineering, fortifying;
To defend their hearths and homes, with patriotic industry,
Fencing every city round with massy walls of masonry;
Tactical devices old they modify with new design;
Arms offensive and defensive to perfection they refine;
Galleys are equipt and arm'd, and armies train'd to discipline.
Look to life, in every part; in all they practise, all they know,
Every nation has derived its best instruction from the foe. 380
    Cho. We're agreed to grant a hearing; if an enemy can teach
Anything that's wise or useful, let him prove it in his speech.
    Pei. (aside). Let's retire a pace or two; you see the change in their behaviour.
    Hoo. Simple justice I require, and I request it as a favour.
    Cho. Faith and equity require it, and the nation hitherto
Never has refused to take direction and advice from you.
    Pei. (aside). They're relenting by degrees;
        Recover arms and stand at ease.
    Cho.   Back to the rear! resume your station,   400
        Ground your wrath and indignation,
        Sheath your fury, stand at ease!
        While I proceed to question these:
        What design has brought them here?

	Hoh, there, Hoopoe! can't he hear?
Hoo.	What's your question?
Cho.	Who are these?
Hoo.	Strangers from the land of Greece.
Cho.	What design has brought them thence? 410
	What's their errand or pretence?
Hoo.	They come here simply with a view
	To settle and reside with you;
	Here to remain and here to live.
Cho.	What is the reason that they give?
Hoo.	A project marvellous and strange.
Cho.	Let us hear him! let us hear him! 432
	Bid him begin! for rais'd on high
	Our airy fancy soars; and I
	Am rapt in hope, ready to fly.

Hoo. (*to the Chorus*). Here you, take these same arms, in the name of Heaven,
And hang them quietly in the chimney-corner; (*turning to Peithetairus,*)
And you, communicate your scheme, exhibiting
Your proofs and calculations—the discourse
Which they were call'd to attend to.
 Pei.   No, not I,
By Jove! unless they agree to an armistice;   440
Such as the little poor baboon, our neighbour,
The sword cutler, concluded with his wife;

That they shan't bite me, or take unfair advantage
In any way.
    Cho.   We won't.
    Pei.   Well, swear it then!
    Cho. We swear, by our hope of gaining the first prize
With the general approval and consent
Of the whole audience, and of all the judges—
And if we fail, may the reproach befall us,
Of gaining it only by the casting vote.
    [*Her.*] *Hoo.* Hear ye, good people all! the troops are order'd
To take their arms within doors; and consult
On the report and entry to be made
Upon our journal of this day's proceedings.   450
    Cho.   Since time began
             The race of Man
      Has ever been deceitful, faithless ever.
        Yet may our fears be vain!
        Speak therefore and explain:
        If in this realm of ours,
    Your clearer intellect searching and clever,
        Has noticed means or powers
          Unknown and undetected,
    In unambitious indolence neglected,
    Guide and assist our ignorant endeavour:
    You, for your willing aid and ready wit,
    Will share with us the common benefit.   460
Now speak to the business and be not afraid,
The Birds will adhere to the truce that we made.

Pei. I'm fill'd with the subject and long to proceed—
My rhetorical leaven is ready to knead.
Boy, bring me a crown and a basin and ewer.
    Eu. Why, what does he mean? Are we banqueting, sure?
    Pei. A rhetorical banquet I mean; and I wish
To serve them at first with a sumptuous dish,
To astound and delight them. "The grief and compassion
That oppresses my mind on beholding a nation,
A people of sovereigns"......   470
    Cho.   Sovereigns we!
    Pei. Of all the creation! of this man and me,
And of Jupiter too; for observe that your birth
Was before the old Titans, and Saturn, and Earth.
    Cho. And Earth!
    Pei.   I repeat it.
    Cho.   That's wonderful news!
    Pei. Your wonder implies a neglect to peruse
And examine old Æsop, from whom you might gather
That the lark was embarrass'd to bury his father

On account of the then non-existence of Earth;
And how, to repair so distressing a dearth,
He adopted a method unheard of and new.
    Cho. If the story you quote is authentic and true,
No doubt can exist of our clear seniority,
And the gods must acknowledge our right to authority.
    Eu. Your beaks will be worn with distinction and pride;
The woodpecker's title will scarce be denied;
And Jove the pretender will surely surrender.   480
    Pei.......Moreover, most singular facts are combined
In proof that the birds were adored by mankind:
For instance, the Cock was a sovereign of yore
In the empire of Persia, and rul'd it before
Darius's time; and you all may have heard
That his title exists as the "Persian bird."...

    Observe that Peithetairus never vouchsafes an answer or takes any kind of notice of his companion, but proceeds continuously, except once or twice in reply to the Chorus.

ACT I.

Eu. And hence you behold him stalk in pride,
Majestic and stout, with a royal stride,
With his turban upright, a privilege known
Reserv'd to kings and kings alone.
    Pei.......So wide was his empire, so mighty his sway,
That the people of earth to the present day,
Attend to his summons and freely obey:
Tinkers, tanners, cobblers, all,
Are roused from rest at his royal call,
And shuffle their shoes on before it is light,
To trudge to the workshop.
    Eu.   I warrant you're right;
I know to my cost, by the cloak that I lost,
It was owing to him I was robb'd and beguil'd.
    For a feast had been made for a neighbour's child,
To give it a name; and I went as a guest,
And sat there carousing away with the rest;
But drinking too deep, I fell soundly asleep;
And he began crowing; and I never knowing,
But thinking it morning, went off at the warning,
(With the wine in my pate, to the city gate),
And fell in with a footpad, was lying in wait,
Just under the town, and was fairly knock'd down;

Then I tried to call out; but before I could shout,
He stripp'd me at once with a sudden pull,
Of a brand new mantle of Phrygian wool.
 Pei.......Then the Kite was the monarch of Greece heretofore....
 Hoo. Of Greece?   500
 Pei.   ...and instructed our fathers of yore,
On beholding a kite to fall down and adore....
 Eu. Well, a thing that befel me, was comical quite,
I threw myself down on beholding a kite;
But turning my face up to stare at his flight,
With a coin in my mouth, forgetting my penny,
I swallow'd it down, and went home without any.
 Pei........At an era, moreover, of modern date,
Menelaus the king, Agamemnon the great,
Had a bird as assessor attending in state,
Perch'd on his sceptre, to watch for a share   510
Of fees and emoluments, secret or fair.
 Nay, Jupiter now that usurps the command
Appears with an Eagle, appointed to stand
As his emblem of empire; a striking example
Of authority once so extended and ample:
And each of the gods had his separate fowl,
Apollo a Hawk, and Minerva an Owl.
 Cho. That's matter of fact, and you're right in the main;
But what was the reason I wish you'd explain.
 Pei. The reason was this: that the bird should be there
To demand as of right a proportional share

Of the entrails and fat; when an offering was made,
A suitable portion before them was laid:
Moreover you'll find that the race of mankind
Always swore by a bird; and it never was heard
That they swore by the gods at the time that I mention. 520
And Lampon himself, with a subtle intention
Adheres to the old immemorial use;
He perjures and cheats us, and swears "by the goose."
    Thus far forth have I prov'd and shown
The power and estate that were once your own
Now totally broken and overthrown:
And need I describe your present tribe,
Weak, forlorn, expos'd to scorn,
Distress'd, oppress'd, never at rest,
Daily pursued with outrage rude,
With cries and noise of men and boys,
Screaming, hooting, pelting, shooting.
The fowler sets his traps and nets,
Twigs of bird-lime, loops, and snares,
To catch you kidnapp'd unawares.
Even within the temple's pale,
They set you forth for public sale,
Paw'd and handled most severely; 530
And, not content with roasting merely,
In an insolent device,
Sprinkle you with cheese and spice;
With nothing of respect or favour,
Derogating from your flavour.
Or for a further outrage have ye
Sous'd in greasy sauce and gravy.

Hoo. Sad and dismal is the story,
　　Human stranger, which you tell,　　540
　Of our fathers' ancient glory
　　Ere the fated empire fell.
　From the depth of degradation
　　A benignant happy fate
　Sends you to restore the nation,
　　To redeem and save the state.
　I consign to your protection,
　　Able to preserve them best,
　All my objects of affection,
　　My wife, my children, and my nest.
Explain then the method you mean to pursue
To recover our empire and freedom anew.
For thus to remain in dishonour and scorn,
Our life were a burthen no more to be borne.
　Pei. Then I move, that the birds shall in common repair
To a centrical point, and encamp in the air;　　550
And intrench and enclose it, and fortify there;
And build up a rampart impregnably strong,
Enormous in thickness, enormously long,
Bigger than Babylon, solid and tall,
With bricks and bitumen, a wonderful wall.
　Eu. Bricks and bitumen! I'm longing to see
What a daub of a building the city will be!
　Pei.......As soon as the fabric is brought to an end,
A herald or envoy to Jove we shall send,
To require his immediate prompt abdication;
And if he refuses, or shows hesitation,
Or evades the demand, we shall further proceed
With legitimate warfare, avow'd and decreed;
With a warning and notices, formally given,
To Jove, and all others residing in heaven,
Forbidding them ever to venture again
To trespass on our atmospheric domain,

With scandalous journies, to visit a list
Of Alcmenas and Semeles; if they persist,
We warn them that means will be taken moreover
To stop their gallanting and acting the lover.
  Another ambassador also will go
Dispatch'd upon earth, to the people below,
To notify briefly the fact of accession,
And enforcing our claims upon taking possession;
With orders in future, that every suitor,
Who applies to the gods with an offering made,
Shall begin with a previous offering, paid
To a suitable Bird, of a kind and degree
That accords with the god, whosoever he be.
In Venus's fane if a victim is slain,   565
First let a Sparrow be feasted with grain.
When gifts and oblations to Neptune are made,
To the Drake let a tribute of barley be paid.
Let the Cormorant's appetite first be appeas'd,
And let Hercules then have an Ox for his feast.
If you offer to Jove, as the sovereign above,
A ram for his own, let the Golden-crown,
As a sovereign bird, be duly preferr'd
Feasted and honour'd, in right of his reign,
With a jolly fat pismire offer'd and slain.
    Eu. A pismire, how droll! I shall laugh till I burst!
Let Jupiter thunder and threaten his worst!   570
    Cho. Then reckon on us for a number and force;
As on you we rely for a ready resource,
In council and policy trusting to you
To direct the design we resolve to pursue.
    Hoo. That's well, but we've no time, by Jove! to loiter,
And dawdle and postpone like Nicias.   640

We should be doing something. First however
I must invite you to my roosting place,
This nest of mine, with its poor twigs and leaves.
And tell me what your names are?
  Pei.   Certainly;
My name is Peithetairus.
  Hoo.   And your friend?
  Eu. Euelpides from Thria.
  Hoo.   Well, you're welcome—
Both of ye.
  Pei. We're oblig'd.
  Hoo.   Walk in together.
  Pei. Go first then, if you please.
  Hoo.   No, pray move forward.
  Pei. But bless me—stop, pray—just for a single moment—
Let's see—do tell me—explain—how shall we manage
To live with you—with a person wearing wings?
Being both of us unfledg'd?   650
  Hoo. Oh! don't be alarm'd; we'll give you a certain root
That immediately promotes the growth of wings.
  Pei. Come, let's go in then; Xanthias, do you mind,
And Manodorus, follow with the bundles.
  Cho. Holloh!
  Hoo.   What's the matter?
  Cho.   Go in with your party,
And give them a jolly collation and hearty.
But the Bird to the Muses and Graces so dear,

The lovely, sweet Nightingale, bid her appear,
And leave her amongst us, to sport with us here.   660
   Pei. (*with a hurried, nervous eagerness*).
O yes, by Jove! indeed, you must indulge them;
Do, do me the favour; call her from the thicket!
For heaven's sake—let me entreat you—bring her here,
And let us have a sight of her ourselves.
   Hoo. (*with grave good-breeding*).
Since it is your wish and pleasure, it must be so;
Come here to the strangers, Procne! show yourself!
   The NIGHTINGALE *enters from the bush.*
   Pei. O Jupiter! what a graceful, charming bird!
And what an attire she wears, all bright with gold!   670
   Eu. Well I should like to kiss her for my part.
   Pei. You blockhead! With that beak she'd run you through.
   Eu. By Jove, then, one must treat her like an egg;
Just clear away the shell and kiss her—thus.
   Hoo. (*disapprovingly*). Let's go.
   Pei.   Go first, then, and good luck go with us.
                                                [*Exeunt.*
   Cho. O lovely sweet companion meet,
   From morn to night my sole delight,
   My little happy gentle mate,

>   You come, you come, O lucky fate! 680
>   Returning here with new delight,
>   To charm the sight, to charm the sight,
>   And charm the ear.
>   Come, then, anew combine
>   Your notes in harmony with mine,
>   And with a tone beyond compare
>   Begin your Anapæstic air.

Ye Children of Man! whose life is a span,
Protracted with sorrow from day to day,
Naked and featherless, feeble and querulous,
Sickly calamitous creatures of clay!
Attend to the words of the Sovereign Birds,
(Immortal, illustrious, lords of the air,)
Who survey from on high, with a merciful eye,
Your struggles of misery, labour, and care.
Whence you may learn and clearly discern
Such truths as attract your inquisitive turn; 690
Which is busied of late with a mighty debate,
A profound speculation about the creation,
And organical life, and chaotical strife,
With various notions of heavenly motions,
And rivers and oceans, and valleys and mountains,
And sources of fountains, and meteors on high,
And stars in the sky...We propose by-and-by,
(If you'll listen and hear,) to make it all clear,
And Prodicus henceforth shall pass for a dunce,
When his doubts are explain'd and expounded at once.

>   Before the creation of Æther and Light,
>   Chaos and Night together were plight
>   In the dungeon of Erebus foully bedight.

ACT I.

Nor Ocean, or Air, or Substance was there,
Or solid or rare, or figure or form,
But horrible Tartarus ruled in the storm.
   At length, in the dreary chaotical closet
Of Erebus old, was a privy deposit,
By Night the primæval in secrecy laid—
A mystical egg, that in silence and shade
Was brooded and hatch'd, till time came about,
And Love, the delightful, in glory flew out,
In rapture and light, exulting and bright,
Sparkling and florid, with stars in his forehead,
His forehead and hair, and a flutter and flare,
As he rose in the air, triumphantly furnish'd
To range his dominions on glittering pinions,
All golden and azure, and blooming and burnish'd:
   He soon, in the murky Tartarean recesses,
With a hurricane's might, in his fiery caresses
Impregnated Chaos; and hastily snatch'd
To being and life, begotten and hatch'd,
The primitive Birds: but the Deities all,   700
The celestial Lights, the terrestrial Ball,
Were later of birth, with the dwellers on earth
More tamely combined, of a temperate kind;
When chaotical mixture approach'd to a fixture.
   Our antiquity proved, it remains to be shown
That Love is our author and master alone;
Like him we can ramble, and gambol and fly
O'er ocean and earth, and aloft to the sky;
And all the world over, we're friends to the lover,
And when other means fail, we are found to prevail
When a Peacock or Pheasant is sent as a present.

All lessons of primary daily concern
You have learnt from the Birds, and continue to learn.
Your best benefactors, and early instructors,
We give you the warning of seasons returning.
When the Cranes are arranged, and muster afloat
In the middle air, with a creaking note,
Steering away to the Libyan sands,   710
Then careful farmers sow their lands;
The crazy vessel is haul'd ashore,
The sail, the ropes, the rudder, and oar
Are all unshipp'd, and housed in store.
    The shepherd is warn'd, by the Kite reappearing,
To muster his flock, and be ready for shearing.
    You quit your old cloak at the Swallow's behest,
In assurance of summer, and purchase a vest.
    For Delphi, for Ammon, Dodona, in fine
For every oracular temple and shrine,
The Birds are a substitute equal and fair,
For on us you depend, and to us you repair
For counsel and aid when a marriage is made,
A purchase, a bargain, a venture in trade:
Unlucky or lucky, whatever has struck ye,
An ox or an ass that may happen to pass,
A voice in the street, or a slave that you meet,
A name or a word by chance overheard,   720
If you deem it an omen, you call it a *Bird;*

And if birds are your omens, it clearly will follow
That birds are a proper prophetic Apollo.

Then take us as gods, and you'll soon find the odds,
We'll serve for all uses, as prophets and muses;
We'll give ye fine weather, we'll live here together;
We'll not keep away, scornful and proud, a-top of a cloud,
(In Jupiter's way); but attend every day
To prosper and bless all you possess,
And all your affairs, for yourselves and your heirs. 730
And as long as you live, we shall give
You wealth and health, and pleasure and treasure,
In ample measure;
And never bilk you of pigeon's milk
Or potable gold; you shall live to grow old,
In laughter and mirth, on the face of the earth,
Laughing, quaffing, carousing, boozing,
 Your only distress shall be the excess
 Of ease and abundance and happiness.

Semichorus.

 Muse that in the deep recesses
  Of the forest's dreary shade,
 Vocal with our wild addresses,
  Or in the lonely lowly glade 740
 Attending near, art pleased to hear
  Our humble bill, tuneful and shrill;
 When to the name of omnipotent Pan
  Our notes we raise, or sing in praise
 Of mighty Cybele, from whom we began,
  Mother of nature and every creature.

>Wing'd or unwing'd, of birds or man;
>Aid and attend, and chaunt with me
>The music of Phrynichus, open and plain,
>The first that attempted a loftier strain,
>Ever busy like the bee, with the sweets of harmony. 750

Epirrhema.

Is there any person present sitting a spectator here,
Who desires to pass his time freely without restraint or fear?
Should he wish to colonize, he never need be check'd or chid
For the trifling indiscretions which the testy laws forbid.
   Parricides are in esteem; among the birds we deem it fair,
A combat honourably fought betwixt a game-cock and his heir!
There the branded runagate, branded and mottled in the face,
Will be deem'd a motley bird; a motley mark is no disgrace. 761
   Spintharus, the Phrygian born, will pass a muster there with ease,
Counted as a Phrygian fowl, and even Execestides,
Once a Carian and a slave, may there be nobly born and free,
Plume himself on his descent, and hatch a proper pedigree.

Semichorus.

>Thus the Swans in chorus follow,   770
> On the mighty Thracian stream
> Hymning their eternal theme—
>Praise to Bacchus and Apollo:

The welkin rings with sounding wings,
With songs and cries and melodies,
Up to the thunderous Æther ascending.

Whilst all that breathe on earth beneath,
The beasts of the wood, the plain, and the flood,
In panic amazement are crouching and bending,
With the awful qualm of a sudden calm
Ocean and air in silence blending.
The ridge of Olympus is sounding on high,   780
Appalling with wonder the lords of the sky,
And the Muses and Graces,
Enthroned in their places,
Join in the solemn symphony.

Antepirrhema.

Nothing can be more delightful than the having wings to wear!
A spectator sitting here, accommodated with a pair,
Might for instance (if he found a tragic chorus dull and heavy)
Take his flight and dine at home, and if he did not choose to
  leave ye,
Might return in better humour when the weary drawl was ended.
Introduce then wings in use—believe me, matters will be
  mended.
Trust me, wings are all in all! Diitrephes has mounted quicker
Than the rest of our aspirants, soaring on his wings of wicker
Basket work and crates and hampers first enable him to fly:
First a captain, then promoted to command the cavalry;
With his fortunes daily rising, office and preferment new,
An illustrious, enterprising, airy, gallant Cockatoo.   800

ACT II.

SCENE: *In the Clouds. A hastily constructed altar stands in the centre of the stage. Enter* PEITHETAIRUS *and* EUELPIDES.

    Pei. Well, there it is! Such a comical set out,
By Jove, I never saw!
    Eu.   Why, what's the matter?
What are you laughing at?
    Pei.   At your pen feathers;
I'll tell ye exactly now the thing you're like;
You're just the perfect image of a Goose,
Drawn with a pen in a writing-master's flourish.
    Eu. And you're like a pluck'd Blackbird to a tittle.
    Pei. Well, then, according to the line in Æschylus,
"It's our own fault, the feathers are our own."
    [*Eu.*] *Cho.* Come, what's to be done?

[*Enter the* HOOPOE.]

    [*Hoo.*] *Pei.*   First we must choose a name,
Some grand, sonorous name, for our new city;
Then we must sacrifice.
    Eu.   I think so too.
    [*Pei.*] *Cho.* Let's see—let's think of a name—what shall it be?
    Pei. What say ye to the Lacedæmonian name?
Sparta sounds well—suppose we call it Sparta.

Eu.   Sparta! What *Sparto?*—Rushes!—no, not I,
I'd not put up with *Sparto* for a mattress,
Much less for a city; we're not come to that.
  Pei.   Come, then, what name shall it be?
  Eu.   Something appropriate,
Something that sounds majestic, striking, and grand,
Alluding to the clouds and the upper regions.
  Pei.   What think ye of Clouds and Cuckoos? Cuckoo-
      cloudlands
Or Nephelococcugia?
  [*Hoo.*] *Cho.*   That will do;
A truly noble and sonorous name!   820
  Eu.   It will be a genteelish, smart concern, I reckon,
This city of ours.—Which of the deities
Shall we have for a patron? We must weave our mantle,
Our sacred mantle, of course—the yearly mantle—
To one or other of 'em.
  Pei.   Well, Minerva?
Why should not we have Minerva? She's establish'd,
Let her continue; she'll do mighty well.
  Eu.   No—there I object; for a well order'd city
The example would be scandalous, to see
The goddess, a female born, in complete armour   830
From head to foot, and Cleisthenes with a distaff.
  Pei.   What warden will ye appoint for the Eagle tower,
Your Citadel, the fort upon the rock?
  [*Hoo.*] *Cho.*   That charge will rest with a chief of our own
      choice,
Of Persian race, a chicken of the game,
An eminent warrior.
  Eu.   Oh my chicky-biddy!
My little master! I should like to see him
Strutting about and roosting on the rock.

Pei. Come you now! please to step to the atmosphere,
And give a look to the work, and help the workmen;
And between whiles, fetch bricks and tiles, and such like;
Draw water, stamp the mortar,—do it barefoot;
Climb up the ladders; tumble down again;   840
Keep constant watch and ward; conceal your watch-lights;
Then go the rounds, and give the countersign,
Till you fall fast asleep. Send heralds off,
—A brace of them—one to the gods above,
And another, down below there, to mankind.
Bid them, when they return, inquire for me.
   Eu. For me! for me! You may be hang'd for me. [*Exit.*
   Pei. Come, friend, go where I bid you; never mind;
The business can't go on without you, any how.
It's just a sacrifice to these new deities,
That I must wait for, and the priest that's coming.
Holloh, you boy there! bring the basin and ewer! [*Exit.* 850
   Cho. We urge, we exhort you, and advise,
     To ordain a mighty sacrifice;
     And before the gods to bring
     A stupendous offering;
     Either a sheep or some such thing!
       To please the critics of the age,
       Sacrificed upon the stage.
       Sound amain the Pythian strain!
     Let Chæris be brought here to sing.

ACT II.

Chæris, a bad musician, is called for, to complete the shabbiness of the performance. His representative, the Crow (who is the Chæris among birds) sounds some discordant notes, till Peithetairus stops him.

Enter PEITHETAIRUS *with a* PRIEST.

Pei. Have done there with your puffing—Heaven and Earth,
What's here? I've seen a many curious things, 860
But never saw the like of this before,
A Crow with a flute and a mouthpiece. Priests, your office:
Perform it! Sacrifice to the new deities!
  Priest. I will—but where's the boy gone with the basket?
      Let us pray to the holy flame,
      And the holy Hawk that guards the same;
      To the sovereign Deities,
      All and each, of all degrees,
      Female and male!
Pei. [*Cho.*] Hail thou Hawk of Sunium, hail!
Priest.   To the Delian and the Pythian Swan,
      And to the Latonian Quail, 870
      All hail!
  [*Cho.*]   To the Bird of awful stature,
      Mother of Gods, mother of Man;
Pei. [*Cho.*]   Great Cybele! nurse of Nature!
      Glorious Ostrich, hear our cry,
      Fearful and enormous creature,
      Hugest of all things that fly,
      O preserve and prosper us
      Thou mother of Cleocritus;
Priest. [*Cho.*]   Grant the blessings that we seek
      For us and for the Chians eke!
  Pei. That's right, the Chians—don't forget the Chians! 880

Priest. To the Heroes, Birds, and Heroes' sons,
We call at once, we call and cry, To the Woodpecker, the Jay, the Pie,
To the Mallard, and the Widgeon, To the Ringdove and the Pigeon,
To the Petrel and Sea-mew, To the Dottrel and Curlew,
To the Vultures and the Hawks, To the Cormorants and Storks,
To the Rail, to the Quail, To the Peewit, to the Tomtit—

Peithetairus, who can do every thing better than every body else, undertakes to perform the sacrifice.

Pei. Have done there! call no more of 'em; are you mad?
Inviting all the Cormorants and Vultures,   890
For a victim such as this! Why don't you see,
A Kite at a single swoop would carry it off?
Get out of my way there with your Crowns and Fillets!
I'll do it myself. I'll make the sacrifice!   [*Exit Priest.*

Cho.   Then must I commence again,
           In a simple humble strain;
           And invite the gods anew,
           To visit us—but very few—
           Or only just a single one,   900
              All alone
           In a quiet easy way;
        Wishing you may find enough,
           If you dine with us to-day;
              Our victim is so poor and thin,
              Merely bones, in fact, and skin.

Pei. We sacrifice and pray to the winged deities.

Enter a POET, *very ragged and shabby, with a mellifluous, submissive, mendicatory demeanour.*

Poet.   "For the festive, happy day,
           Muse, prepare an early lay
           To Nephelococcugia."

Pei. What's here to do? What are you? Where do you come from?

Poet. An humble menial of the Muses' train,
As Homer expresses it.
Pei. A menial, are you,
With your long hair? A menial?
Poet. 'Tis not that,
No!—but professors of the poetical art
Are simply styled, the "Menials of the Muses,"
As Homer expresses it.
Pei. Ay, the Muse has given you
A ragged livery. Well, but friend, I say—
Friend! Poet! What the plague has brought you here?
Poet. I've made an Ode upon your new-built City,
And a charming composition for a Chorus,
And another in Simonides's manner.
Pei. (*in a sharp cross-examining tone*). When were they made?
What time? How long ago?
Poet. From early date, I celebrate in song
The noble Nephelococcugian state.
Pei. That's strange, when I'm just sacrificing here,
For the first time, to give the town a name.
Poet. Intimations swift as air
To the Muses' ear are carried,
Swifter than the speed and force
Of the fiery-footed horse;
Hence, the tidings never tarried;
Father, patron, mighty lord,
Founder of the rising state,
What thy bounty can afford,
Be it little, be it great,
With a quick resolve incline
To bestow on me and mine.
Pei. This fellow will breed a bustle, and make mischief,

If we don't give him a trifle, and get rid of him.
You there, you've a spare waistcoat; pull it off! [*To a slave.*
And give it this same clever ingenious poet—
There, take the waistcoat, friend. Ye seem to want it!
    Poet.   Freely, with a thankful heart,
        What the bounteous hand bestows
      Is received in friendly part;
        But amid the Thracian snows,
        Or the chilly Scythian plain,
          He the wanderer, cold and lonely,
          With an under-waistcoat only,
      Must a further wish retain;
        Which the Muse averse to mention,
        To your gentle comprehension
      Trusts her enigmatic strain.
  Pei. I comprehend it enough; you want a jerkin.
Here, give him yours; one ought to encourage genius.
There, take it, and good-bye to ye!
    Poet.   Well, I'm going;
And, as soon as I get to the town, I'll set to work;
And finish something, in this kind of way:
    "Seated on your golden throne,   950
      Muse, prepare a solemn ditty
        To the mighty,
        To the flighty,
      To the cloudy, quivering, shivering,
      To the lofty seated city."   [*Exit Poet.*

Pei. Well, I should have thought that jerkin might have
    cured him
Of his "quiverings and shiverings." How the plague
Did the fellow find us out? I should not have thought it.
  Come, once again, go round with the basin and ewer.
Peace! Silence, silence!

Enter a SOOTHSAYER, *with a great air of arrogance and self-
importance.*

Sooth.   Stop the sacrifice!
Pei. What are you?   960
Sooth.   A Soothsayer, that's what I am.
Pei. The worse luck for ye.
Sooth.   Friend, are you in your senses?
Don't trifle absurdly with religious matters.
Here's a prophecy of Bakis, which expressly
Alludes to Nephelococcugia.
Pei. How came it, then, you never prophesied
Your prophecies, before the town was built?
Sooth. The spirit withheld me.
Pei.   And is it allowable now,
To give us a communication of them?
Sooth.   Hem!
    "Moreover, when the Crows and Daws unite,
    To build and settle in the midway, right
    Between tall Corinth and fair Sicyon's height,   970
    Then to Pandora let a milk white Goat
    Be slain and offer'd, and a comely coat
    Given to the soothsayer, and shoes a pair;
    When he to you this oracle shall bear."

Pei. Are the shoes mention'd?
Sooth. (*pretending to feel for his papers*). Look at the book, and see!
  "And let him have the entrails for his share."
Pei. Are the entrails mention'd?
Sooth. (*as before*).　　　Look at the book, and see!
  "If you, predestined youth, shall do these things,
  Then you shall soar aloft, on eagle's wings;
  But, if you do not, you shall never be
  An Eagle, nor a Hawk, nor bird of high degree."
Pei. Is all this there?　　　　　　　　　　　　980
Sooth. (*as before*).　　　Look at the book, and see!
Pei. This oracle differs most remarkably
From that which I transcribed in Apollo's temple.
  "If at the sacrifice......which you prepare,
  An uninvited vagabond......should dare
  To interrupt you, and demand a share,
  Let cuffs and buffets......be the varlet's lot.
  Smite him between the ribs......and spare him not."
Sooth. Nonsense you're talking!
Pei. (*with the same action as the Soothsayer, as if he were feeling for papers*).　　　Look at the book, and see!
  "Thou shalt in no wise heed them, or forbear
  To lash and smite those Eagles of the air,
  Neither regard their names, for it is written,
  Lampon and Diopeithes shall be smitten."
[*Sooth.* Is all this there?
Pei. (*producing a horsewhip*). Look at the book, and see!]
Get out, with a plague and a vengeance.　　　990
Sooth.　　　　　　　　　Oh dear! oh!
Pei. Go soothsay somewhere else, you rascal, run!
　　　　　　　　　　　　[*Exit Soothsayer.*

ACT II.

METON *the Astronomer appears, encumbered with a load of mathematical instruments.*

Met. I'm come, you see, to join you—
Pei. (aside). (Another plague!)
For what? What's your design? Your plan, your notion?
Your scheme,—your apparatus,—your equipment—,
Your outfit? What's the meaning of it all?
Met. I mean to take a geometrical plan
Of your atmosphere—to allot it, and survey it
In a scientific form.
Pei. In the name of heaven!
Who are ye and what? What name? What manner of man?
Met. Who am I and what? Meton's my name, well known
In Greece, and in the village of Colonos.
Pei. (going up to him). But tell me, pray, these implements,
these articles,
What are they meant for?
Met. These are—*Instruments!*
An atmospherical geometrical scale.
First, you must understand, that the atmosphere   1000
Is form'd,—in a manner,—altogether,—partly,
In the fashion of a furnace, or a funnel;
I take this circular arc, with the moveable arm,
And so, by shifting it round, till it coincides
At the angle—you understand me?
Pei. Not in the least.
Met. (with animation)........I obtain a true division, with the
quadrature
Of the equilateral circle. Here, I trace
Your market place, in the centre, with the streets
Converging inwards,—and the roads, diverging
From the circular wall, without—like solar rays
From the circular circumference of the Sun.

Pei. (in a pretended soliloquy; then calling to him with a tone of mystery and alarm).
Another Thales! absolutely, a Thales!
Meton! 1010
   Met. (startled). Why, what's the matter?
   Pei. You're aware
That I've a regard for you. Take my advice;
Don't be seen here—Withdraw yourself; abscond!
   Met. Is there any alarm or risk?
   Pei. Why, much the same
As it might be in Lacedæmon. There's a bustle
Of expelling aliens; people are dragg'd out
From the inns and lodgings, with a deal of uproar,
And blows and abuse in plenty, to be met with
In the public streets.
   Met. A popular tumult—heh?
   Pei. (scandalized at the supposition). Oh, fie! no, nothing of that kind.
   Met. How do you mean then?
   Pei. We're carrying into effect a resolution
Adopted lately; to discard and cudgel
Coxcombs and Mountebanks of every kind.
   Met. Perhaps I had best withdraw.
   Pei. Why yes, *perhaps*—
But yet, I would not answer for it, neither;
Perhaps, you may be too late; the blows I mention'd
Are coming—close upon you—there they come! [*Striking him.*
   Met. Oh bless me!
   Pei. Did not I tell you, and give you warning?
Get out, you coxcomb, find out by your Geometry
The road you came, and measure it back; you'd best. 1020
[*Exit Meton.*

A COMMISSIONER *from Athens advances with an air of importance and ascendancy.*
   Com. Is nobody here? None of the Proxeni,

ACT II.

To receive and attend upon me?
    Pei.   What's all this?
Sardanapalus in person come amongst us!
    Com.   I come, appointed as Commissioner
To Nephelococcugia.
    Pei.   A Commissioner!
What brings you here?
    Com.   A paltry scrap of paper,
A trifling silly decree, that sent me away
Here to this place of yours.
    Pei.   Well now! suppose,
To make things easy on both sides—could not you
Just take your salary at once; and so return,
Without any further trouble?
    Com.   Truly yes,
I've other affairs at home: a speech and a motion,
That I meant to have made in the general assembly,
About a business that I took in hand
On the part of my friend Pharnaces, the satrap.
    Pei. Agreed then, and farewell. Here, take your salary.
    Com. What's here?   1030
[*Peithetairus has held out his left hand as if with an offer of money, he grasps the right hand of the Commissioner, and with this advantage proceeds to buffet him.*]
    Pei.   A motion on the part of Pharnaces!
    Com. Bear witness here! I'm beaten and abused
In my character of Commissioner!   [*Exit* COMMISSIONER.
    Pei.   Get out!
With your balloting-box and all. It's quite a shame,
Quite scandalous! They send commissioners here,
Before we've finish'd our first sacrifice.
Enter a HAWKER *with copies of new laws relating to the colony, which he has brought out with him, for sale.*
    Haw. "Moreover, if a Nephelococcugian

Should assault or smite an Athenian citizen"—
Pei. What's this? What's all this trumpery paper here?
Haw. I've brought you the new laws and ordinances,
And copies of the last decrees to sell.
Pei. (dryly and bitterly). Let's hear 'em.
Haw. "It's enacted and ordain'd,
That the Nephelococcugians shall use
Such standard weights and measures"— 1040
Pei. Friend, you'll find
Hard *measure* here, and a heavy *weight*, I promise you,
Upon your shoulders shortly.
Haw. What's the matter? What's come to you?
Pei. Get out, with your decrees!
I've bloody decrees against you, dire decrees. [*Drives him off.*
Com. (returning). I summon Peithetairus to his answer,
In an action of assault and battery,
For the first day of the month Munychion.
Pei. Hah! say you so? You're there again! Have at you. [*Drives him off.*
Haw. (returning). "And in case of an assault or violence,
Against the person of the Magistrate"— 1050
Pei. Bless me! What you! You're there again.
[*Drives him off.*
Com. (returning again). I'll ruin you;
I'll lay my damages at ten thousand drachmas.
Pei. In the mean time, I'll smash your balloting boxes.
Com. Remember, how you effaced the public monument
On the pillar, and defil'd it, late last night.
Pei. Pah! stuff! There, seize him, somebody. What you're off, too.
Come, let's remove, and get away from hence,
And sacrifice our goat to the Gods within doors.
[*Exeunt all but Chorus.*

ACT II.

Chorus.

Henceforth—our Worth,
Our Right—our Might,
Shall be shewn,
Acknowledg'd, known;
Mankind shall raise
Prayers, vows, praise,
To the Birds alone.   1060
Our employ, is to destroy
The vermin train,
Ravaging amain
Your fruits and grain:
We're the wardens
Of your gardens,
To watch and chase
The wicked race,
And cut them shorter
In hasty slaughter.   1070

Epirrhema.

At the present urgent crisis, all your efforts and attention
Are directed to secure Diagoras's apprehension:
Handsome bounties have been offer'd of a talent for his head,
Likewise with respect to Tyrants (Tyrants that are gone and dead)
Bounties of a talent each, for all that can be kill'd or caught.
With a zealous emulation, we, the Birds, have also thought
Just and proper to proclaim, from this time forth, that we withdraw
From Philocrates, the fowler, the protection of the law:
Furthermore, we fix a price for bringing him alive or dead:
Four, if he's secured alive; a single talent for his head:
He, that Ortolans and Quails to market has presumed to bring,
And the Sparrows, six a penny, tied together in a string, 1081

With a wicked heart retaining sundry Doves in his employ,
Fasten'd with their feet in fetters, forced to serve for a decoy.
Farther, we declare and publish our command to men below,
All the Birds you keep in prison, to release and let them go.
We shall, else, revenge ourselves, and we shall teach the tyrants
    yet,
How to chirp and dance in fetters, in the tangles of a net.

CHORUS.

    Blest are they,
    The Birds alway,
    With perfect clothing,
    Fearing nothing,   1090
Cold or sleet or summer heat.
    As it chances,
    As he fancies,
Each his own vagary follows,
Dwelling in the dells and hollows;
When, with eager weary strain,
The shrilly grasshoppers complain,
Parch'd upon the sultry plain,
Madden'd with the raging heat;
We secure a cool retreat,
In the shady nooks and coves,
Recesses of the sacred groves,
Many an herb, and many a berry
Serves to feast, and make us merry.   1100

ANTEPIRRHEMA.

To the judges of the prize, we wish to mention in a word
The return we mean to make, if our performance is preferr'd.

First, then, in your empty coffers you shall see the sterling
    Owl,
From the mines of Laurium, familiar as a common fowl;
Roosting among the bags and pouches, each at ease upon his
    nest;
Undisturb'd rearing and hatching little broods of interest: 1108
If you wish to cheat in office, but are inexpert and raw,
You should have a Kite for agent, capable to gripe and claw;
Cranes and Cormorants shall help you to a stomach and a throat
When you feast abroad. But if you give a vile, unfriendly vote,
Hasten and provide yourselves, each, with a little silver plate,
Like the statues of the gods, for the protection of his pate;
Else, when forth abroad you ramble on a summer holiday,
We shall take a dirty vengeance, and befoul your best array.

Enter PEITHETAIRUS.

Pei. Well, Friends and Birds, the sacrifice has succeeded;
Our omens have been good ones, good and fair.
But what's the meaning of it? We've no news
From the new building yet! No messenger!   1120
Oh! there at last, I see,—There's somebody
Running at speed, and panting like a racer.

Enter a MESSENGER *quite out of breath, and speaking in short
snatches.*

  Mess. Where is he? Where? Where is he? Where?
    Where is he?—
The president, Peithetairus?
  Pei. (*coolly*).   Here am I.
  Mess. (*in a gasp for breath*). Your fortification's finish'd.

Pei. Well! that's well.
Mess. A most amazing, astonishing work it is!
So that Theagenes and Proxenides
Might flourish, and gasconade, and prance away,
Quite at their ease, both of them four-in-hand,
Driving abreast upon the breadth of the wall,
Each in his own new chariot.
Pei. You surprise me.
Mess. And the height (for I made the measurement myself)
Is exactly a hundred fathom. 1131
Pei. Heaven and earth!
How could it be? Such a mass! Who could have built it?
Mess. The Birds; no creature else—no foreigners,
Egyptian bricklayers, workmen or masons,
But they themselves alone, by their own efforts
(Even to my surprise, as an eye-witness)—
The Birds, I say, completed everything.
There came a body of thirty thousand Cranes
(I won't be positive, there might be more)
With stones from Africa in their craws and gizzards,
Which the Stone-curlews, and Stone-chatterers
Work'd into shape and finish'd. The Sand-Martins,
And Mud-larks, too, were busy in their department,
Mixing the mortar, while the Water-Birds, 1140
As fast as it was wanted, brought the water
To temper, and work it.
Pei. (*in a fidget*). But who served the masons?
Who did you get to carry it?
Mess. To carry it?
Of course the Carrion Crows, and Carrying Pigeons.
Pei. Yes! yes! But after all, to load your hods—

How did you manage that?
    Mess.   Oh, capitally,
I promise you.—There were the Geese, all barefoot,
Trampling the mortar, and, when all was ready,
They handed it into the hods so cleverly
With their flat feet!
    Pei.   They *footed* it, you mean.
Come; it was handily done though, I confess.
    Mess. Indeed, I assure you, it was a sight to see them;
And trains of Ducks there were clambering the ladders,
With their duck legs, like bricklayer's 'prentices,   1150
All dapper and handy, with their little trowels.
    Pei. In fact, then, it's no use engaging foreigners;
Mere folly and waste; we've all within ourselves.
Ah, well now, come! But about the woodwork? Heh!
Who were the carpenters? Answer me that!
    Mess. The Woodpeckers, of course: and there they were,
Labouring upon the gates, driving and banging,
With their hard hatchet beaks, and such a din,
Such a clatter as they made, hammering and hacking,
In a perpetual peal, pelting away
Like shipwrights hard at work in the arsenal.
And now their work is finish'd, gates and all,
Staples and bolts, and bars, and everything;
The sentries at their posts; patrols appointed;   1160
The watchmen in the barbican; the beacons
Ready prepared for lighting; all their signals
Arranged—But I'll step out, just for a moment,
To wash my hands.—You'll settle all the rest.
                                              [*Exit Messenger.*

Peithetairus remains in an attitude of perplexity and astonishment.

    CHORUS (*to Peithetairus, in a self-satisfied tone*).
Heighday! Why, what's the matter with ye? Sure!
Ah! well now, I calculate, you're quite astonish'd;

You did not know the nature of our birds:
I guess you thought it an impossible thing
To finish up your fortification job
Within the time so cleverly.
 Pei. (*recovering himself and looking round*). Yes, truly.
Yes, I'm surprised, indeed, I must confess—
I could almost imagine to myself
It was a dream, an illusion altogether—
But there's the watchman of the town, I see,
In alarm and haste it seems! He's running here—
   [*The* WATCHMAN *enters, with a shout of alarm.*   1170
Well, what's the matter?
 W.   A most dreadful business!
One of the Gods just now—Jupiter's Gods—
Has bolted through the gates and driven on
Right into the atmosphere, in spite of us,
And all the Jackdaws, that were mounting guard.
 Pei. (*animated at the prospect of having something to manage*).
What an outrage! What an insult! Which of 'em?
Which of the Gods?
 Watchman.   We can't pretend to say;
We just could ascertain that he wore wings.
We're clear upon that point.
 Pei.   But a light party
Ought surely to have been sent in such a case;
A detachment—
 Watchman.   A detachment has been sent
Already a squadron of ten thousand Hawks,   1180
Besides a corps of twenty thousand Hobby-hawks,
As a light cavalry, to scour the country;
Vultures and Falcons, Ospreys, Eagles, all
Have sallied forth; the sound of wings is heard,

ACT II.   55

Rushing and whizzing round on every side
In eager search. The fugitive divinity
Is not far off, and soon must be discover'd.
   Pei. Did nobody think of slingers? Where are they?
Where are the slingers got to? Give me a sling.
Arrows and slings, I say!—Make haste with 'em.

                   CHORUS.

       War is at hand,
       On air and land,
         Proclaim'd and fix'd.
       War and strife,
       Eager and rife,
         Are kindled a-twixt
      This state of ours,
      And the heavenly powers.
       Look with care   1190
      To the circuit of air;
       Watch lest he,
       The Deity,
     Whatever he be,
       Should unaware
     Escape and flee.

But, hark! The rushing sound of hasty wings
Approaches us. The deity is at hand.

       Enter IRIS, *flying across the scene.*

   Pei. Holloh, you! Where are ye flying? Where are ye
      going?
Hold! Halt! Stop there, I tell ye!—Stop this instant! 1200
What are ye? Where do you come from? Speak, explain.
   Iris. Me? From the Gods, to be sure! the Olympian Gods.
   Pei. (*pointing to the flaunting appendages of her dress*).
What are ye with all your flying trumpery?
A helmet, or a galley? What's your name?
   Iris. Iris, the messenger of the Gods.
   Pei.   A messenger!
Oh, you're a naval messenger, I reckon:
The Salaminian galley, or the Paralian?

You're in full sail, I see.
   Iris. What's here to do?
   Pei. Are there no birds in waiting? Nobody
To take her into custody?
   Iris. Me—to custody?
Why, what's all this?
   Pei. You'll find to your cost, I promise ye.
   Iris. Well, this seems quite unaccountable!
   Pei. Which of the gates
Did ye enter at, ye jade? How came you here?
   Iris. Gates!—I know nothing about your gates, not I.
   Pei. Fine innocent ignorant airs she gives herself! 1211
You applied to the Pelicans, I suppose?—The captain
Of the Cormorants on guard admitted you?
   Iris. Why, what the plague! what's this?
   Pei. So you confess!
You came without permission!
   Iris. Are you mad?
   Pei. Did neither the sitting magistrates nor bird-masters
Examine and pass you?
   Iris. Examine me, forsooth!
   Pei. This is the way then!—without thanks or leave
You ramble and fly, committing trespasses
In an atmosphere belonging to your neighbours!
   Iris. And where would you have us fly then? Us, the
      Gods!
   Pei. I neither know nor care.—But I know this— 1220
They sha'n't fly here.—And another thing I know;
I know that, if there ever was an instance

Of an Iris or a rainbow, such as you,
Detected in the fact, fairly condemn'd,
And justly put to death, it would be you.
    Iris. But I'm immortal.
    Pei. (*coolly and peremptorily*). That would make no difference;
We should be strangely circumstanced indeed,
With the possession of a Sovereign Power,
And you, the Gods, in no subordination,
No kind of order, fairly mutinying,
Infringing and disputing our commands.
Now then, you'll please to tell me where you're going?
Which way you're steering with those wings of yours?
    Iris (*in a great fright, but attempting to assume a tone of authority*). I?...I'm commission'd from my father Jove
To summon human mortals to perform   1231
Their rites and offerings and oblations, due
To the powers above.
    Pei.   And who do you mean? what powers?
    Iris. What powers? Ourselves, the Olympian Deities!
    Pei. So then, you're deities, the rest of ye!
    Iris. Yes, to be sure; what others should there be?
    Pei. Remember—once for all—that we, the Birds,
Are the only deities from this time forth,
And not your father Jove. By Jove! not he!
    Iris. Oh, rash, presumptuous wretch! Incense no more
The wrath of the angry Gods, lest Ruin drive
Her ploughshare o'er thy mansion; and Destruction,   1240
With hasty besom, sweep thee to the dust;
Or flaming lightning smite thee with a flash,
Left in an instant smouldering and extinct.

Pei. Do ye hear her?—Quite in tragedy!—Quite sublime!
Come, let me try for a bouncer in return.
Let's see.—Let's recollect.—" Me dost thou deem,
Like a base Lydian or a Phrygian slave,
With hyperbolical bombast to scare?"
I tell ye, and you may tell him—Jupiter,
If he provokes me and pushes things too far,
Will see some eagles of mine, to outnumber his,
With firebrands in their claws, about his house.
And I shall send a flight of my Porphyrions,
A hundred covey or more, arm'd *cap-à-pie*,   1250
To assault him in his sublime celestial towers;
Perhaps he may remember, in old times
He found enough to do with one Porphyrion.
Come, scuttle away; convey your person elsewhere;
Be brisk, and leave a vacancy. Brush off.
   Iris. I shall inform my father. He shall know
Your rudeness and impertinence. He shall—
He'll settle ye and keep ye in order.—You shall see. [*Exit Iris.*
   Pei. Oh dear! is it come to that? No, you're mistaken, 1260
Young woman, upon that point; I'm not your man;
I'm an old fellow grown; I'm thunder proof;
Proof against flames and darts and female arts:
You'd best look out for a younger customer.

CHORUS.

    Notice is hereby given
    To the deities of heaven,
      Not to trespass here
      Upon our atmosphere.
    Take notice—from the present day
      No smoke or incense is allow'd
      To pass this way.

   Pei. Quite strange it is! quite unaccountable!
That herald to mankind that was dispatch'd,
What has become of him? He's not yet return'd.   1270

Enter a HERALD.

   Herald. Oh, Peithetairus, happiest, wisest, best,
Cleverest of men! Oh, most illustrious!

Oh, most inordinately fortunate!
Oh, most...Oh, do, for shame, do bid me have done.
   Pei. What are you saying?
   Her.   All the people of Earth
Have joined in a complimentary vote, decreeing
A crown of gold to you, for your exertions.
   Pei. I'm much oblig'd to the people of Earth. But why?
What was their motive?
   Her.   Oh, most noble founder
Of this supereminent, celestial city,
You can't conceive the clamour of applause,
The enthusiastic popularity,
That attends upon your name; th' impulse and stir
That moves among mankind, to colonize
And migrate hither. In the time before,   1280
There was a Spartan mania, and people went
Stalking about the streets with Spartan staves,
With their long hair unwash'd and slovenly,
Like so many Socrateses; but of late
Birds are the fashion—Birds are all in all—
Their modes of life are grown to be mere copies
Of the birds' habits; rising with the Lark;
Scratching and scrabbling suits and informations;
Picking and pecking upon points of law;
Brooding and hatching evidence;—in short,
It has grown to such a pitch, that names of Birds   1290
Are given to individuals; Chærophon,
Is call'd an Owl; Theagenes, a Goose;

Philocles, a Cock Sparrow; Midias,
A Dunghill Cock. And all the songs in vogue   1300
Have something about Birds, Swallows or Doves;
Or about flying, or a wish for wings.
  Such is the state of things, and I must warn you,
That you may expect to see some thousands of them
Arriving here, almost immediately,
With a clamorous demand for wings and claws;
I advise you to provide yourself in time.
    Pei. Come, it won't do then, to stand dawdling here;
Go you, fill the hampers and the baskets there
With wings, and bid the loutish porter bring them,   1310
While I stop here, to encounter the new comers.

Enter a YOUNG MAN (*singing*).

"Oh! for an Eagle's force and might,
  Loftily to soar
Over land and sea, to light
  On a lonely shore."

ACT II. 61

Pei. Well, here's a song that's something to the purpose. 1340
Y. Man. Ay, ay, there's nothing like it—wings and flying!
Wings are your only sort. I'm a bird fancier.
In the new fashion quite. I've taken a notion
To settle and live amongst ye. I like your laws.
    Pei. (*very gravely and methodically*). What laws do you mean?
    We've many laws amongst us.
    Y. Man. Your laws in general; but particularly,
The law that allows of beating one's own father.
    Pei. Why truly, Yes! we esteem it a point of valour
In a Chicken, if he clapperclaws the old Cock. 1350
    Y. Man. That was my view, feeling a wish in fact
To throttle mine, and seize the property.
    Pei. (*with great candour and composure*).
Yes, but you'd find some difficulties here;
An obstacle insurmountable, I conceive;
An ancient statute standing unrepeal'd,
Engraved upon our old Ciconian columns.
It says: that when a Stork, or a Ciconia,
Has brought his lawful progeny of young Storks
To bird's estate, and enabled them to fly,
The sire shall stand entitled to a maintenance,
At the son's cost and charge, in his old age.
    Y. Man (*with a start of disappointment*).
I've managed finely, it seems, to mend myself!
Forced to maintain my father after all!
    Pei. (*in a soothing tone*). No, no; not quite so bad; since
    you're come here, 1360
As a well-wisher to the establishment,
Zealous and friendly, we'll contrive to equip you
With a suit of armour as a soldier's orphan.
And now, young man, let me suggest some notions,
Things that were taught me when a boy. "Your father?

Strike him not!" rather take this pair of wings;
And this cockspur (*giving him a sword*); imagine you've a
 coxcomb
Upon your head, to serve you for a helmet;
Look out for service, and enlist yourself;
Get into a garrison; live upon your pay;
And let your father live. You're fond of fighting,
And fond of flying—take a flight to Thrace;
There you may please yourself, and fight your fill.
 Y. Man. By Jove, you're right. The notion's not a bad one.
I'll follow it up! 1371
 Pei. (*very gravely and quietly*).
  You'll find it the best way. [*Exit Young Man.*
  Enter a SYCOPHANT (*singing*).
  "Tell us who the strangers are,
   Gentle Swallow! Birds of air,
   Party-colour'd, poor and bare, 1410
   Tell us who the strangers are;
   Gentle Swallow, tell me true."
 Pei. Here's a fine plague broke out! See yonder fellow
Sauntering along this way, swaggering and singing.
 Syc. Hoh! gentle Swallow! I say, my gentle Swallow,
My gentle Swallow! How often must I call?
 Pei. Why, there it is; the prodigal in the fable
Seeking for Swallows in a ragged coat.
 Syc. (*in an arrogant, overbearing tone*).
Who's he that's set to serve out wings? Where is he?
 Pei. 'Tis I; but what do you want? You should explain.
 Syc. Wings! Wings! You need not have ask'd me. Wings
  I want. 1420
 Pei. Do you mean to fly for flannel to Pellene?
 Syc. (*a little disconcerted*). No, no! But I'm employ'd...I
  employ myself
In fact, among the allies and islanders;
I'm in the informing line.

Pei. (*in a tone of very grave irony*). I wish you joy.

Syc. And a mover and manager for prosecutions
In criminal suits, and so forth; you understand me;
So I wish to equip myself with a pair of wings
To whisk about and trounce the islanders.

Pei. Would it be doing things in better form
To serve a summons flying, think ye?

Syc. (*not knowing very well what to make of him*). No,
Not that; but just to avoid the risk of pirates,
To return in company with a flight of cranes,
(As they do with the gravel in their gizzards)
With a belly-full of lawsuits for my ballast.

Pei. (*in a grave and somewhat twaddling tone*).
So this is your employment! A young man   1430
Like you to be an informer! Is it possible?

Syc. Why shouldn't it? I was never bred to labour.

Pei. (*as before*). But sure, there are other lawful occupations,
In which a brisk young fellow, such as you,
Might earn an honest, decent livelihood
In credit and good will, without informing.

Syc. (*thoroughly taken in, becomes emphatically insolent*).
Wings, my good fellow!—wings I want—not words!

Pei. (*dryly*). I'm giving you wings already.

Syc. (*a little puzzled*).   What, with words?
Is that your way?

Pei. (*in a tone of very grave banter*).
                Yes, for mankind in general
Are wing'd, as it were, and brought to plume themselves
In different ways, by speeches and discourse.

Syc. (*confused and puzzled*). What, all?

Pei. (*as before*). Yes, all. I'll give you a striking instance:
You must have heard yourself elderly people
Sitting conversing in a barber's shop.
And one says—"Well, Diitrephes has talk'd   1440

So much to my young man, he has brought him at last
To plume himself in driving." And another
Says that his son is quite amongst the clouds,
Grown flighty of late with studying tragedy.

Syc. (*with a sort of hesitating laugh*).
So words are wings, you say.

Pei. No doubt of it.
I say it, and I repeat it; human nature
Is marvellously rais'd and elevated
By words. I was in hopes that I might raise you,
By words of good advice, to another sphere,
To live in an honest calling. 1450

Syc. (*feeling himself bantered and beaten but restive and angry*).
But I won't, though.

Pei. (*coolly*). Why, what will you do?

Syc. (*sulkily at first, but animating as he proceeds*).
Why I won't disgrace my family:
My father, and my grandfather before him,
Served as informers; and I'll stick to it,
The profession.—So you'll please to hand 'em me out,
A pair of your best wings, Vulture's or Hawk's,
To fly to the islands, with my summonses,
And home again to record them in the courts,
And out again to the islands.

Pei. (*in a tone of interest*). Yes, that's well;
I understand ye, I think; your method is,
To be beforehand with 'em? Your defendant,
You get him cast for non-appearance, heh!
Before he can arrive; and finish him
In his absence, heh?

Syc. (*completely taken in, delighted, rubbing his hands*).
By Jove, you're up to it!

Pei. Then, whilst he's sailing here you get the start,
And fly, to pounce upon the property,
To rummage out the chattels. 1460

Syc. That's the trick,

The notion of it!—I see you're up to it.—
A man must whisk about, here and away,
Just like a whipping-top.
 Pei.   Ay, yes, you're right;
I understand you. The instance is a good one.
A whipping-top, you say. Well, by good luck,
I've here a capital, slashing suit of wings
To serve ye, made of a cow-hide from Corcyra.
 Syc. Oh, heaven! what's there? a horsewhip?
 Pei.   Wings, I tell ye.
To whisk ye about; to flog ye and make ye fly.
 Syc. Oh dear! oh dear!
 Pei.   Scamper away, you scoundrel!
Vanish, you vagabond! whisk yourself off!
I'll pay ye for your practices in the courts—
Your pettifoggicorascalities. [*Exit Sycophant.*
 (*To the attendants*)
Come, bundle up the wings; let's take 'em back. [*Exeunt.*

CHORUS.

Strophe.

 We have flown and we have run, 1470
 Viewing marvels many a one,
 In every land beneath the sun.
  But the strangest sight to see
 Was a huge exotic tree,
 Growing, without heart or pith,
 Weak and sappy, like a wyth;
 But with leaves and boughs withal,
 Comely, flourishing, and tall.
  This the learned all ascribe
 To the Sycophantic tribe;
 But the natives there, like us,
 Call it a Cleonymus.
 In the spring's delightful hours
 It blossoms with rhetoric flowers;

I saw it standing in the field,
With leaves in figure like a shield;
On the first tempestuous day   1480
I saw it cast those leaves away.

Antistrophe.

There lies a region out of sight,
Far within the realm of night,
Far from torch and candle-light.
There in feasts of meal and wine
Men and demigods may join;
There they banquet and they dine,
Whilst the light of day prevails;
At sunset their assurance fails.
If any mortal then presumes,   1490
Orestes, sallying from the tombs,
Like a fierce heroic sprite,
Assaults and strips the lonely wight.

Enter PROMETHEUS *muffled up, peeping about him.*

Pro.   Oh, dear! if Jupiter should chance to see me!
Where's Peithetairus?   Where?
   Pei. (*re-entering*).   Why, what's all this?
This fellow muffled up?
   Pro.   Do look behind me;
Is anybody watching? any Gods
Following and spying after me?

Pei.   No, none;
None that I see; there's nobody—But you!
What are ye?
    Pro.   Tell me, what's the time of day?
    Pei. Why, noon; past noon; but tell me, who are ye?
         Speak.   1500
    Pro. Much past? How much?
    Pei. (*aside*).   Confound the fool, I say!
The insufferable blockhead!
    Pro.   How's the sky?
Open or overcast? Are there any clouds?
    Pei. (*aloud and angrily*).
Be hang'd!
    Pro.   Then I'll disguise myself no longer.
                                            (*throws off his cloak.*)
    Pei. My dear Prometheus!
    Pro.   Hold your tongue, I beg;
Don't mention my name! If Jupiter should see me
Or overhear ye, I'm ruin'd and undone.
But now, to give you a full complete account
Of everything that's passing there in Heaven—
The present state of things—But first, I'll trouble you
To take the umbrella, and hold it overhead,
Lest they should overlook us.
    Pei.   What a thought!   1510
Just like yourself! A true Promethean thought!
Stand under it, here! Speak boldly; never fear.
    Pro. D'ye mind me?

Pei.   Yes, I mind ye; speak away.
Pro. (*emphatically*). Jupiter's ruin'd!
Pei.   Ruin'd! How? Since when?
Pro.   From the first hour you fortified and planted
Your atmospheric settlements. Ever since
There's not a mortal offers anything
In the shape of sacrifice.—No smoke of victims!
No fumes of incense! Absolutely nothing!
We're keeping a strict fast—fasting perforce,
From day to day—the whole community.
And the inland barbarous Gods in the upper country   1520
Are broken out, quite mutinous and savage,
With hunger and anger; threatening to come down
With all their force, if Jupiter refuses
To open the ports and allow them a free traffic
For their entrails and intestines, as before.
    Pei. (*a little annoyed at being obliged to ask*).
What, are there other barbarous Gods besides
In the upper country?
    Pro.   Barbarous? To be sure;
They're all of Execestides's kindred.
    Pei. (*as before hesitating, but with a sort of affected ease*).
Well...but...the name now: These same barbarous deities...
What name do you call 'em?
    Pro.   Call them! The Triballi!
    Pei. Ah! well, then, that accounts for our old saying—
Confound the *Tribe* of them!   1530
    Pro. (*drily*).   Precisely so.
But now to business. Thus much I can tell ye—

That envoys will arrive immediately
From Jupiter and those upland wild Triballi,
To treat for a peace. But you must not consent
To ratify or conclude, till Jupiter
Acknowledges the sovereignty of the Birds,
Surrendering up to you the Sovereign Queen,
Whom you must marry.
  Pei.   Why, what Queen is that?
  Pro. What Queen?—A most delightful, charming girl—
Jove's housekeeper, that manages his matters,
Serves out his thunderbolts, arranges everything;
The constitutional laws and liberties,   1540
Morals and manners, the marine department,
Freedom of speech, and threepence for the juries.
  Pei. Why, that seems all in all.
  Pro.   Yes, everything
I tell ye; in having her, you've everything;
I came down hastily to say thus much;
I'm hearty, ye know; I stick to principle.
Steady to the human interest—always was.
  Pei. Yes, we're obliged to you for our roast victuals.
  Pro. And I hate these present Gods you know, most
    thoroughly:
I need not tell you that.
  Pei. (*with a sneer*).   No, no, you need not,
You're known of old for an enemy to the Gods.
  Pro. Yes, yes, like Timon; I'm a perfect Timon;
Just such another. But I must be going;
Give me the umbrella; if Jupiter should see me, 1550
He'll think that I'm attending a procession.
  Pei. That's well; but don't forget the folding chair,
For a part of your disguise. Here, take it with you.
      [*Exit Prometheus followed by Peithetairus.*

ACT III.

SCENE: *as in Act II, except that the gates and walls are seen half-built.* PEITHETAIRUS *standing at a stove, busily engaged in cooking.*

Enter NEPTUNE, *the* TRIBALLIAN ENVOY, HERCULES.

Nep. There's Nephelococcugia, that's the town,
The point we're bound to, with our embassy.
   (*Turning to the Triballian Envoy.*)
But you! What a figure have ye made yourself!
What a way to wear a mantle! slouching off
From the left shoulder! Hitch it round, I tell ye,
On the right side. For shame,—come,—so; that's better,
These folds too, bundled up. There, throw them round
Even and easy,—so. Why, you're a savage,
A natural born savage. Oh, democracy!   1570
What will it bring us to? when such a ruffian
Is voted into an embassy!
   Tri. (*to Neptune who is pulling his dress about*). Come, hands off!
Hands off!
   Nep.   Keep quiet, I tell ye, and hold your tongue,
For a very beast; in all my life in heaven,
I never saw such another. Hercules,
I say, what shall we do? What should you think?
   Her. What would I do? What do I think? I've told you

Already—I think to throttle him—the fellow,
Whoever he is, that's keeping us blockaded.
    Nep. Yes, my good friend; but we were sent, you know,
To treat for a Peace. Our embassy is for peace.
    Her. That makes no difference; or if it does,
It makes me long to throttle him the more.
    Pei. (*very busy, affecting not to see them*).
Give me the Silphium spice. Where's the cheese grater?
Bring cheese here, somebody! Mend the charcoal fire.   1590
    Her. Mortal, we greet you and hail you! Three of us.
Three deities—
    Pei. (*without looking up*). But I'm engaged at present;
A little busy, you see, mixing my sauce.
    Her. Why sure! How can it be? what dish is this?
Birds seemingly!
    Pei. (*without looking up*). Some individual birds,
Opposed to the popular democratic birds,
Render'd themselves obnoxious.
    Her.   So, you've pluck'd them,
And put them into sauce, provisionally?
    Pei. (*looking up*). Oh! bless me, Hercules, I'm quite glad
        to see you!
What brings you here?
    Her.   We're come upon an embassy
From Heaven, to put an end to this same war—
    Serv. (*to Peithetairus*). The cruet's empty, our oil is out.
    Pei.   No matter,
Fetch more, fetch plenty, I tell ye. We shall want it.   1590
    Her.—For, in fact it brings no benefit to us,
The continuance of the War prolonging it;
And you yourselves, by being on good terms

Of harmony with the Gods—why, for the future,
You'd never need to know the want of rain,
For water in your tanks; and we could serve ye
With reasonable, seasonable weather,
According as you wish'd it, wet or dry.
And this is our commission coming here,
As envoys, with authority to treat.
    Pei. Well, the dispute, you know, from the beginning
Did not originate with us. The war
(If we could hope in any way to bring you
To reasonable terms) might be concluded.
Our wishes, I declare it, are for Peace,
If the same wish prevails upon your part;
The arrangement in itself, is obvious.
A retrocession on the part of Jupiter.
The Birds again to be reintegrated   1600
In their estate of sovereignty. This seems
The fair result; and if we can conclude,
I shall hope to see the ambassadors to supper.
    Her. Well, this seems satisfactory; I consent.
    Nep. (*to Hercules*). What's come to ye? What do ye mean?
      Are ye gone mad?
You glutton! would you ruin your own father,
Depriving him of his ancient sovereignty?
    Pei. Indeed!—And would not it be a better method
For all you Deities, and confirm your power,
To leave the Birds to manage things below?
You sit there, muffled in your clouds above,
While all mankind are shifting, skulking, lurking,
And perjuring themselves here out of sight.
Whereas, if you would form a steady strict   1610
Alliance with the Birds, when any man
(Using the common old familiar oath—
"By Jupiter and the crow") forswore himself,
The Crow would pick his eyes out, for his pains.
    Nep. Well, that seems plausible—that's fairly put.
    Her. I think so, too.
    Pei. (*to the Triballian*). Well, what say you?

ACT III. 73

Trib. Say true.
Pei. (*very volubly,—quite at his ease*).
Yes. He consents, you see! But I'll explain now
The services and good offices we could do you.
Suppose a mortal made a vow, for instance,
To any o' You; then he delays and shuffles,
And says, "The Gods are easy creditors." 1620
In such a case, we could assist ye, I say,
To levy a fine.
Nep. How would you do it? Tell me.
Pei. Why, for example, when he's counting money,
Or sitting in the bath, we give the warrant
To a poursuivant of ours, a Kite or Magpie;
And they pounce down immediately, and distrain
Cash or apparel, money or money's worth,
To twice the amount of your demand upon him.
Her. Well, I'm for giving up the sovereignty,
For my part.
Nep. The Triballian, what says he?
Her. (*aside to the Triballian, shewing his fist*).
You, Sir; do you want to be well bang'd or not?
Mind how you vote! Take care how you provoke me.
Trib. Yaw, yaw. Goot, goot.
Her. He's of the same opinion.
Nep. Then, since you're both agreed, I must agree. 1630
Her. (*shouting to Peithetairus*).
Well, you! We've settled this concern, you see,
About the sovereignty; we're all agreed.
Pei. O faith, there's one thing more, I recollect,
Before we part; a point that I must mention.
As for dame Juno, we'll not speak of her;
I've no pretensions, Jupiter may keep her;
But, for that other Queen, his manager,
The sovereign Goddess, her surrender to me

Is quite an article indispensable.
 Nep. (*with gravity and dignity*). Your views, I find, are not
  disposed for peace:
We must turn homewards.
 Pei.   As you please, so be it.
Cook, mind what you're about there with the sauce;
Let's have it rich and savory, thicken it up!
 Her. How now, man? Neptune! are you flying off?
Must we remain at war, here, for a woman?
 Nep. But, what are we to do?   1640
 Her.   Do? Why, make peace.
 Nep. (*in great wrath*). I pity you really! I feel quite
  asham'd
And sorry to see you; ruining yourself!
If anything should happen to your father,
After surrendering the sovereignty,
What's to become of you? When you yourself
Have voted away your whole inheritance;
At his decease, you must remain a beggar.
 Pei. (*aside to Hercules*). Ah there! I thought so; he's coming
  over ye;
Step here, a moment! Let me speak to ye!
Your Uncle's chousing you, my poor dear friend,
You've not a farthing's worth of expectation,
From what your father leaves. Ye can't inherit
By law: ye're illegitimate, ye know.   1650
 Her. Heighday! Why, what do you mean?
 Pei.   I mean the Fact!
Your mother was a foreigner; Minerva
Is counted an heiress, everybody knows;
How could that be, supposing her own father
To have had a lawful heir?

ACT III.   75

Her.   But, if my Father
Should choose to leave the property to me,
In his last Will.
    Pei.   The law would cancel it!
And Neptune, he that's using all his influence
To work upon ye, he'd be the very first
To oppose ye, and oust ye, as the testator's brother.
I'll tell ye what the law says, Solon's law: 1660
    "A foreign heir shall not succeed,
       Where there are children of the lawful breed:
       But, if no native heir there be,
       The kinsman nearest in degree
       Shall enter on the property."
    Her. Does nothing come to me then?—Nothing at all,
Of all my father leaves?
    Pei.   Nothing at all,
I should conceive. But you perhaps can tell me;
Did He, your Father, ever take ye with him,
To get ye enroll'd upon the register?
    Her. No truly, I—thought it strange—he—never did. 1670
    Pei. Well, but don't think things strange. Don't stand
        there, stammering,
Puzzling and gaping. Trust yourself to me,
'Tis I must make your fortune after all!
If you'll reside and settle amongst us here,
I'll make you chief Commander among the Birds,
Captain, and Autocrat and every thing,
Here you shall domineer and rule the roast,
With splendour and opulence and pigeon's milk.
    Her. (*in a more audible voice, and in a formal decided tone*).
I agreed with you before: I think your argument
Unanswerable. I shall vote for the surrender.
    Pei. (*to Neptune*). And what say you?
    Nep. (*firmly and vehemently*).   Decidedly, I dissent.
    Pei. Then it depends upon our other friend,
It rests with the Triballian. What say you?

Tri. Me tell you; pretty girl, grand beautiful Queen,
Give him to Birds.
    Her.   Ay, give her up, you mean.
    Nep. Mean! He knows nothing about it. He means
        nothing   1680
But chattering like a Magpie.
    Pei.   Well, "The Magpies"
He means the Magpies or the Birds in general.
The Republic of the Birds—their government—
That the surrender should be made to them.
    Nep. (*in great wrath*). Well, settle it yourselves; amongst
        yourselves;
In your own style: I've nothing more to say.
    Her. (*to Peithetairus*). Come, we're agreed in fact to grant
        your terms;
But you must come, to accompany us to the sky;
To take back this same Queen, and the other matters.
    Pei. (*very quietly*). It happens lucky enough, with this pro-
        vision
For a marriage feast. It seems prepared on purpose.
    Her. Indeed, and it does. Suppose in the meanwhile,
I superintend the cookery, and turn the roast,
While you go back together.   1690
    Nep. (*with a start of surprise and disgust*). Turn the roast!
A pretty employment! Won't you go with us?
    Her. No thank ye; I'm mighty comfortable here.
    Pei. Come, give me a marriage robe; I must be going.
                [*Exeunt Peithetairus and the three gods.*

                Interval.

HARBINGER *or* HERALD, *announcing the approach of Peithetairus.*
    O fortunate! O triumphant? O beyond
        All power of speech or thought, supremely blest,

Prosperous happy Birds!—Behold your King,
Here in his glorious palace!—Mark his entrance,
Dazzling all eyes, resplendent as a Star;
Outshining all the golden lights, that beam, 1710
From the rich roof, even as a summer Sun,
Or brighter than the Sun, blazing at Noon.
  He comes; and at his side a female form
Of beauty ineffable; wielding on high,
In his right hand, the winged thunderbolt,
Jove's weapon. While the fumes of incense spread,
Circling around and subtle odours steal
Upon the senses from the wreathed smoke,
Curling and rising in the tranquil air.
See, there He stands! Now must the sacred Muse
Give with auspicious words her welcome due.

Semichorus.

Stand aside and clear the ground, 1720
Spreading in a circle round
With a worthy welcoming;
To salute our noble King
In his splendour and his pride,
Coming hither side by side,
With his happy lovely bride.
O the fair delightful face!
What a figure! What a grace!
What a presence! What a carriage!
What a noble worthy marriage!
Let the Birds rejoice and sing,
At the wedding of the King;
Happy to congratulate
Such a blessing to the state. 1730
      Hymen Hymen Hoh!

>
> Jupiter, that God sublime,
> When the Fates, in former time,
> Match'd him with the Queen of Heaven,
> At a solemn banquet given,
> Such a feast was held above;
> And the charming God of Love,
> Being present in command,
> As a Bridesman took his stand,   1740
> With the golden reins in hand.
>   Hymen Hymen Hoh!

Pei. I accept and approve the marks of your love,
Your music and verse I applaud and admire.

Chorus.

[*Pei.*] But raise your invention, and raising it higher,
Describe me the terrible engine of Jove,
The thunder of Earth and the thunder above.

[*Cho.*] O dreaded Bolt of Heaven,
The Clouds with horror cleaving,
And ye terrestrial thunders deep and low   1750
Closed in the subterranean caves below,
That even at this instant growl and rage,
Shaking with awful sound this earthly stage;
Our King by you has gain'd his due;
By your assistance, yours alone,
Everything is made his own,
Jove's dominion and his throne;
And his happiness and pride,
His delightful lovely bride.
                 Hymen Hymen Hoh!

[*Pei.* Birds of ocean and of air,
Hither in a troop repair,
To the royal ceremony,
Our triumphant matrimony!
 Come for us to feast and feed ye!
  Come to revel dance and sing!—
 Lovely creature! Let me lead ye
  Hand in hand, and wing to wing.]

P.S. *The numbering of the lines is that of Meineke, which is followed also in the acting edition.*

TRANSLATION OF THE PARABASIS.

(ll. 685—723.)

By A. C. SWINBURNE.

Come on then, ye dwellers by nature in darkness, and like to
    the leaves' generations,
That are little of might, that are moulded of mire, unenduring
    and shadowlike nations,
Poor plumeless ephemerals, comfortless mortals, as visions of
    shadows fast fleeing,
Lift up your mind unto us that are deathless, and dateless the
    date of our being:
Us, children of heaven, us, ageless for aye, us, all of whose thoughts
    are eternal;
That ye may from henceforth, having heard of us all things
    aright as to matters supernal,
Of the being of birds and beginnings of gods, and of streams, and
    the dark beyond reaching,

Truthfully knowing aright, in my name bid Prodicus pack with his
 preaching.
  It was Chaos and Night at the first, and the blackness of darkness,
   and Hell's broad border,
Earth was not, nor air, neither heaven; when in depths of the
 womb of the dark without order
First thing first-born of the black-plumed Night was a wind-egg
 hatched in her bosom,
Whence timely with seasons revolving again sweet Love burst out
 as a blossom,
Gold winds gleaming forth of his back, like whirlwinds gustily
 turning.
He, after his wedlock with Chaos, whose wings are of darkness, in
 Hell broad-burning,
For his nestlings begat him the race of us first, and upraised us
 to light new-lighted.
And before this was not the race of the gods, until all things by
 Love were united:
And of kind united with kind in communion of nature the sky
 and the sea are
Brought forth, and the earth, and the race of the gods everlasting
 and blest. So that we are
Far away the most ancient of all things blest. And that we
 are of Love's generation
There are manifest manifold signs. We have wings, and with us
 have the Loves habitation;
And manifold fair young folk that forswore love once, ere the
 bloom of them ended,

Have the men that pursued and desired them subdued, by the help of us only befriended,
With such baits as a quail, a flamingo, a goose, or a cock's comb staring and splendid.
 All best good things that befall men come from us birds, as is plain to all reason;
For first we proclaim and make known to them spring, and the winter and autumn in season:
Bid sow, when the crane starts clanging for Afric, in shrill-voiced emigrant number,
And calls to the pilot to hang up his rudder again for the season, and slumber;
And then weave cloak for Orestes the thief, lest he strip men of theirs if it freezes.
And again thereafter the kite reappearing announces a change in the breezes,
And that here is the season for shearing your sheep of their spring wool. Then does the swallow
Give you notice to sell your greatcoat, and provide something light for the heat that's to follow.
Thus are we as Ammon, or Delphi, unto you, Dodona, nay, Phœbus Apollo.
For, as first ye come all to get auguries of birds, even such is in all things your carriage,
Be the matter a matter of trade, or of earning your bread, or of any one's marriage.
And all things ye lay to the charge of a bird that belong to discerning prediction:

Winged fame is a bird, as you reckon: you sneeze, and the sign's as a bird for conviction:

All tokens are "birds" with you—sounds too, and lackeys, and donkeys. Then must it not follow

That we ARE to you all as the manifest godhead that speaks in prophetic Apollo?

www.ingramcontent.com/pod-product-compliance
Lightning Source LLC
Chambersburg PA
CBHW020301090426
42735CB00009B/1170